my new filing technique is unstoppable

david rees

Riverhead Books

New York

RIVERHEAD BOOKS

Published by The Berkley Publishing Group

A division of Penguin Group (USA) Inc.

375 Hudson Street

New York, New York 10014

First Riverhead trade paperback edition: March 2004

Library of Congress Cataloging-in-Publication Data

Rees, David, 1972–
      My new filing technique is unstoppable / David Rees.—1st Riverhead trade pbk. ed.
         p. cm.
      ISBN 1-57322-382-4
    I. Title.

  PN6727.R384M94 2004
  741.5'973—dc22

                                                    2004041771

Printed in the United States of America
10 9 8 7 6 5 4 3 2

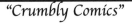

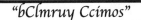
"bClmruy Ccimos"

Bad news guys! The competition's got a filing technique that makes ours look like a **total piece of crap!**

YOU GODDAMN FUCKING SON OF A BITCH! DON'T YOU *EVER* TALK SHIT ABOUT OUR FILING TECHNIQUE!!!

Yeah! It's alphabetical!!!

We've got all the letters lined up in the classic order: Just say, "*A, B, C, D...*" **For fuck's sake, what could be easier to remember?**

And... what could be easier to be TOTALLY AWESOME???

So the best we can do is file everything according to some musty 5,000-year-old alphabet? That's pathetic!!!

!!!

But nothing beats alphabetical order! IT'S THE ONLY ORDER LETTERS COME IN!

Fuck alphabetical order! I want a system that nobody else has! Like, I was thinking—what if we arranged numbers using one computer but then *filed shit* according to how **another** computer secretly calculated them? The competition would have a heart attack from that shit!

Am I the only man with the courage to dream of a brighter tomorrow?

This motherfucker has lost his mind. Bye.

Time-Share Comics

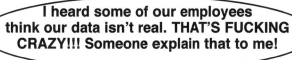

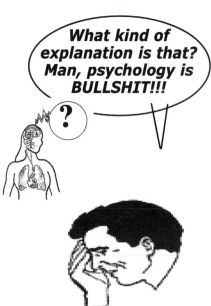

"CRUMBLY COMICS"

Another day, another damn dollar! Another dollar, another damn day! Where does this journey **end**?

At least I'm alone with my pile-file. Maybe I can get some work done.

YOU! How long have you been standing there? No doubt spying on my pile-file, eh?

Boing!
Triangle Body Mode! Somebody better get the fuck out of my office before somebody gets fired! Thank you very much!!!

I love **Triangle Body Mode!** I call it my "Snooping Motherfucker Removal Service!"

"Crombly Comocs"

"THE FILES COME OUT AT NIGHT"

A knock at my office door! That means someone is going to talk my ear off about crappy bullshit I don't understand!

...May I help you?

You have the best pile of notebooks in the whole office! What's your... secret?

Inquiring minds want to **steal!**

?????

I'm sorry, but the secret of my "pile of notebooks" is too intense to share with you. Let's just say it's more than a **pile**—it's also a **file**! So can you please leave me in peace with a **smile??**

*Before I spring a classical Triangle Body Mode experience on your ass and make your life suck by a **mile?***

It's official! *Symptom:* He thinks his **pile** is a **file!** *Diganosis:* Crazy ol' grumpy motherfucker.

Goddammit! Why can't we figure out his fucking filing system? *IT'S SITTING RIGHT THERE!!!*

"CRUMBLY COMICS"

"Profiles in Filing"

"CRUMBLY COMICS"

"OFFICE DAZE"

"CRUMBLY COMICS"

Huh—my database shows a big increase in filing errors. Wonder what that's all about? OH WELL, FORGET IT.

Hey! Wanna walk to that filing protocol meeting together?

FUCK!!! I totally forgot about that fucking stupid meeting... So guess what? *I'm not going!!!*

That's funny you say that, because the meeting is **MANDATORY!**

Please leave me in peace, pokey-headed mother-fucker. I have real work to do.

That's funny you say that, because it's not like you're the only person who has work to **DO!**

Later: "A vision of boredom."

Now this particular filing technique is very interesting. You can see from the bar graph how effective it is.

I like this one better than the other one!

FUCK!!! Why do I have to be at this dumb meeting? Thank God for my laptop—I'm working on my projects.

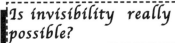

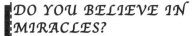

"Crumbly Comics"

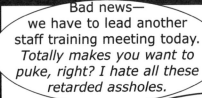

"crumbly comics"

Did you finish the derivative file yesterday?

NO I DID NOT! DERIVATIVE FILES SUCK!!!

PRINT-GOO 9

No wonder this report is so fucked up! Would you please tell me the next time you're not gonna do your job?

WOULD YOU PLEASE TELL ME THE NEXT TIME YOU PLAN ON BEING DUMB? I ASSUME IT WILL BE EVERY MOMENT OF YOUR LIFE.

OK, how can I make her feel as bad as I feel?

Sweet revenge... so sweet yet sour

I'm gonna fart on her spreadsheet and forward her files to an empty bucket!

meanwhile.....

WHAT ARE YOU PEOPLE DOING IN MY OFFICE? THE SIGN SAYS "FOXY LADIES ONLY!"

We're all foxy ladies in God's eyes. But we're having a meeting and you're not invited.

So it's agreed: the most dangerous motto is "If life is a beach, then work is the poisonous sand that ruins the fun!" Let's track it down AND KILL IT.

KILL ALL MOTTO MAKERS

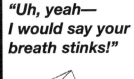
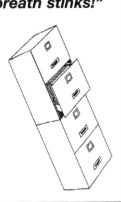

SYNTAX ERROR

LARRY!!!

HAVE YOU SEEN MY LAPTOP COMPUTER?

TODAY I HAVE A BIG MEETING AND I NEED MY LAPTOP COMPUTER!!!

YEAH, I'VE GOT YOUR LAPTOP COMPUTER-- COME INTO MY ROOM AND SEE WHAT I'VE DONE WITH IT!!!

BEEP BEEP! LET'S DOWNLOAD OUR DATA FILES! XASDFJKL!

"A LESSON FROM MR. COMPUTER SCIENCE"

(page 45)

"CRUMBLY COMICS"

Where the hell is my account? I'm missing ten thousand dollars this morning!!!

That account was deleted. It's OK because you have other accounts. **HAVE A GREAT DAY BYE!!!!**

NO YOU DIDN'T! PICK YOUR PHONE BACK UP!!! *HELLO???*

What are you screaming about in here? You wrinkled my printout.

Jesus, man. I log on to my account this morning and it disappears and then I call the lady and she hangs up on me!

Why do you think I'm trying to start my own company using these stolen printouts???

I can't wait until they capture whoever is stealing all the printouts!

Totally!

COME ON, PRINTOUTS!!! HELP ME MAKE A NEW LIFE!!!

"CHICKEN POT PIE MASTERPIECE THEATRE"

"CRUBLY COICS"

So, are you scared about the new filing technique?

WHAT?

Oh, didn't you hear? They're making a new filing technique that uses ONLY NUMBERS.

Tell me you're joking! I'm still struggling with the old technique!

1-9
10-19
18-19
50-53

L-E
M-K
I-N
O-?!

I wish I was joking, but these assholes can't go two days without coming up with another ridiculous fuckin' stupid-ass idea—WHOA, WHAT'S THIS?

WHAT???

Oh man, if you compare this amazing, beautiful bar graph to that crappy pie chart bullshit "Mr. Pie Chart" makes, you will see the difference between perfection and two million piles of manure.

Lemme see! Maybe we could submit it for a "Courage of Perfection" award!

Jesus, will she ever shut up about that dumb award?

What an amazing bar graph!

Thank you! Did you see my data?

WHAT THE FUCK???

Could you please light some scented candles? I need to have a nervous breakdown. **A BAR GRAPH IS TALKING TO ME**

Sure! Anything for my SECRET LOVER!

The only bar graph I need... is to wear cool shades!

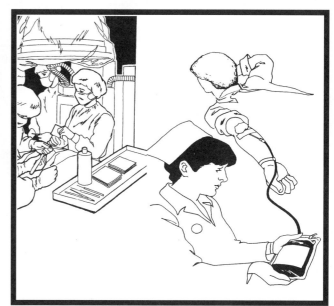

"CRUMBLY COMICS"

29405393780317272787